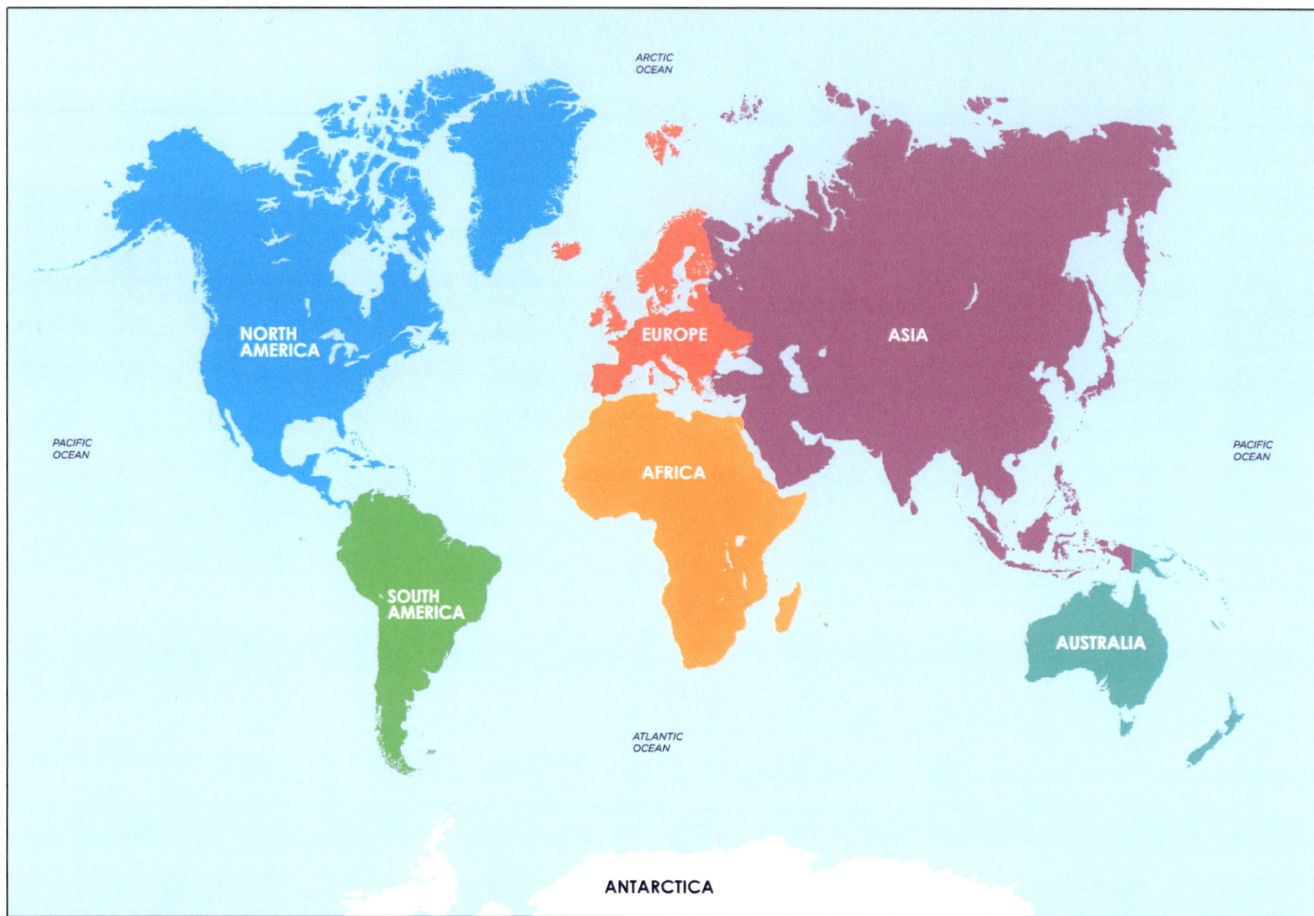

Printed in the United States of America

First Printing, 2024

ISBN 978-0-9913285-3-6

EXP PhotoART Inc.
2301 Sun Valley Drive
Delafield, WI 53018

Our Feathered Friends Around The World

An A To Z Book Of Birds

Photography By
Adel B. Korkor, MD

Written By
Kathleen S. Sampson, RN, MSN

EXP PhotoART Inc.
Delafield, Wisconsin

Special thanks for Mr. Nick Resheske for his help in designing
the book's layout and its production.

Interested in more photography by Adel B. Korkor, M.D.?
Please visit Purity Photography at *www.purityphotos.com*.

DEDICATION

I am dedicating this book to Aziza, an African Grey Parrot who was part of my life for over thirty years. Photography has been my hobby for years and photographing birds has become my passion. I am so fascinated by these feathered creatures. Birds are nature's magic in action. This book is in honor of the numerous comforting moments Aziza gave me.

Aziza chose me as "her man" and would start singing and fluttering her wings as soon as I stepped into the house. She took showers, walked around the house, and sang with me. Not infrequently, she would taste my morning coffee and snatch some of my breakfast cereal.

Aziza, your love has transformed me into a "bird nerd"!

This book is for you.

With forever love,

Adel

A

Agami Heron

South America is this bird's usual home. Agami Herons have short legs and quite a long beak that looks like a sword. These special features make them expert fishermen from the edge of lakes and rivers.

B

Bluebird

Bluebirds live in North America. Did you know they have an amazing ability to spot insects 50 yards away, even in tall grass? Males, without a mate, can sing up to 1,000 songs per hour to attract a mate.

C

Chinstrap Penguin

Can you see the black line under their chin that looks like a helmet strap? Chinstrap Penguins live in the freezing cold water of the Antarctic region. They build their nest with stones which helps prevent melting snow from running into their nest and getting the baby chicks wet. Other penguins will try to steal stones from each other's nests, so they need to be on alert for would-be burglars!

Dusky Sunbird

Dusky Sunbirds live in Africa. They have a long beak to help them eat nectar from flowers. The nest is built in about one week by only the female bird. She will use spider webbing to attach the back of the nest to tree branches or between the thorns of a prickly-pear cactus.

E

Eastern Great Egret

This Egret lives in Asia, Australia, and the islands in that area. Their beak is yellow during the breeding season while they look for a mate, then the beak turns black. Their neck is one and a half times as long as its own body, that is very long!

F

American Flamingo

Flamingos are very funny when they eat! They twist their head and beak upside down in the water to suck up water filled with tiny animals and plants. Then they filter and pump the water out the sides of their beak, keeping the tiny animals and plants for a tasty meal.

Grey Crowned Crane

The Great Crowned Crane lives in Africa and is one of the rarest birds in the world. They are spectacular dancers with bobbing heads and wings fluttering. Did you know the chicks are 'precocial'? Precocial means the baby chicks can run as soon as they hatch.

H

Hooded Merganser

Hooded Mergansers are amazing underwater swimmers. These birds can remain underwater for two minutes while chasing a fish for dinner! Once they have the fish, they resurface and turn the fish around to always swallow it headfirst. This method will avoid injury from the spiny fins of the fish.

I

Indigo Bunting

Indigo Buntings are highly dimorphic. Dimorphic means the male and female colors are very different. The male Indigo Bunting is a beautiful, blue jewel-like color, while the female is a dull brown. Did you know Indigo Buntings do not actually have blue pigment in their feathers? Rather, the blue color of the feathers comes from tiny structures in the feathers that reflect blue light, much like the particles that cause the sky to look blue.

J

White-Necked Jacobian

This hummingbird lives in Mexico and South America. When they fly, they spread their tails open like a fan to help them hover and search for insects. Did you know some females will trick the male hummingbirds by keeping her feathers a dazzling blue and white color, just like their male's feathers? This trick will fool the male bird into thinking she is male too! Then, he will less likely chase her away from food sources.

K

King Penguin

These 3 feet tall birds live in the islands surrounding Antarctica. This bird does not build a nest! Instead, both the mom and dad King Penguin take turns, for about 3 months, balancing the egg or baby chick on their feet in a "brood pouch". The brood pouch keeps the egg and baby chick safe and warm.

L

Long Bill Curlew

This bird is the largest shorebird in North America. Curlews have a long-curved bill, about eight inches long. They use the long bill to poke under soil and mud looking for insects, worms and spiders that have burrowed deeply.

M

Mute Swan

Did you know Mute Swans are a monogamous couple? This means they bond as a pair with each other for life. The Mute Swan is one of the heaviest birds; they average about 20–25 pounds. Despite their heavy weight, they can fly as fast as 50 miles per hour!

N

Northern Mocking Bird

Do you know where the mockingbird got its name? It is from their impressive vocal talent! They can mock the songs of hundreds of other birds, imitate man-made noises like music and machinery, and make sounds like 12 different frogs.

O

Whooping Crane

Did you know Whooping Cranes are the tallest birds in North America? They stand 5 feet tall and have a wingspan of 7 feet. These cranes are the rarest crane species, there are only 600 birds left in the world. They are also monogamous and have the same mate for life.

P

Peregrine Falcon

This falcon lives on every continent except Antarctica. Did you know that a Peregrine Falcon can dive up to an amazing 200 miles per hour to capture its prey in flight? They strike their prey in midair with outstretched talons, or claws.

Q

Gambel's Quail

Worldwide quails live in woodlands and forests, but the Gamble's Quail lives in the desert of the southwest USA. To avoid their predators, they stay in large groups and will join a dozen other quails to walk or run along the ground in groups called coveys. They scratch for food under shrubs and cacti, eating grass and their favorite cactus fruits.

Redhead Duck

Redhead Ducks are diving ducks that eat only plants and leaves. Did you know they can dive as deep as 15 feet? Redhead Ducks make some strange noises! The drake (male) sounds like a cat's meow or purr and the female (hen) will quack! The hen will often share a nest with another Redhead Duck or lay her eggs in either another duck or bird's nest.

S

Snowy Owl

Snowy Owls are monogamous couples and have the same mate for life. The female will sit on the eggs to keep them warm and safe until they hatch. Meanwhile, her mate will feed her. Did you know most owls are nocturnal? Nocturnal means they sleep during the day and hunt at night. The Snowy Owl is diurnal, which means they are active during the day.

T

Tufted Titmouse

Did you know the Tufted Titmouse does not migrate? Instead, it remains in the same home area all-year round. They make their nest in tree holes, but they cannot make their own nesting cavity hole. Instead, they use an old hole leftover by a woodpecker.

U

Red-Breasted Nuthatch

Did you know they can climb headfirst down a tree trunk? Their foot has one big toe (hallux) that faces backwards and three other toes that face forward. The big hallux toe holds them firmly to tree bark as they climb down headfirst in search of insects that are hidden in the tree bark. They hide food, like seeds, in tree bark and on the ground to eat later, and some of those seeds grow into trees.

V

Village Weaver

This bird lives in Africa. Did you know this is the only bird that can tie knots? The males are the nest builders. They weave and tie knots to make the best nest to attract a mate. A group of male birds will build a large village of nests, weaving as many as 100 nests in a single tree.

W

Wood Duck

Did you know Wood Duck chicks are precocial? Precocial means the ducklings will hatch with feathers and are ready to swim the next day. After the ducklings hatch, they must jump to the ground or water from their very high nest inside a tree cavity, then the mother raises the ducklings in the water. They are one of the few ducks that can perch in a tree because their webbed feet have sharp nails.

Cedar Waxwing

Cedar Waxwings are nomadic and spend a lot of time in flocks. Nomadic means they do not migrate, rather they move around in big flocks to areas that have plenty of food and water. Their favorite food is fruit, especially cedar berries. Cedar Waxwings will wait to build their nests until late summer when fruits are ripened and plentiful.

Yellow-Headed Amazon

This bird is in the parrot family. Did you know a unique ability of parrots is to use their feet to bring food to their beak to feed? The Yellow-Headed Amazon is different from other parrots. It will fly 40 miles per hour quietly and silently, rather than squawking and calling out in flight.

Z

Australian Zebra Finch

Did you wonder where this finch got their name? Yes, they have stripes like a "zebra"! Their beaks are black when they are born and change to red or orange as they grow older and mature. The females do not sing, but males have a beautiful song. Australian Zebra Finches are quite social and live in large flocks of 100 or more.

www.ingramcontent.com/pod-product-compliance
Lightning Source LLC
Chambersburg PA
CBRC101308020426
42333CB00008B/79